PERFORMANCE
EDITIONS

DEBUSSY
Seven Favorite Pieces

Edited and Recorded by Christopher Harding

T0071642

To access companion recorded performances online, visit:
www.halleonard.com/mylibrary

Enter Code
6938-3112-4084-3553

On the cover:
Waterlilies, (1916–19) (oil on canvas)
by Monet, Claude
(1840–1926)

Musée Marmottan Monet, Paris, France / The Bridgeman Art Library

ISBN 978-1-4584-6266-4

G. SCHIRMER, *Inc.*
DISTRIBUTED BY
HAL•LEONARD®
7777 W. BLUEMOUND RD. P.O. BOX 13819 MILWAUKEE, WI 53213

www.halleonard.com

CONTENTS

The price of this publication includes access to companion recorded performances online, for download or streaming, using the unique code found on the title page. Visit **www.halleonard.com/mylibrary** and enter the access code.

PERFORMANCE NOTES

TOWARD AN UNDERSTANDING OF PLAYING THE MUSIC OF CLAUDE DEBUSSY

Style

In studying Debussy's music, our attention to detail and the interpretation of his markings must be as meticulous as when we approach the music of Haydn and Mozart. Debussy had a real abhorrence of pianists who performed his music with cavalier freedom. On several occasions he expressed his desire for a faithful interpreter, one who would not yield to the temptation of doing what is not written, in the indulgence of "personal interpretation." It is true that we can't (and should not) avoid real differences of performance among us, but we must strive to create in our minds an exact understanding of what is written.

An example of this might be the "railroad tracks" or "double dashes" we find at the end of certain passages marked with tempo fluctuations (i.e., "cedez", mm. 11, 23 and 27 in "La fille aux cheveux de lin"). These dashes indicate that the cedez is finished and does not imply a break in the sound or a lift of the hand from the keyboard as might be assumed in other styles of music. (Other specific details, especially of articulation, are treated below.)

This emphasis on the exact and precise nature of his music is very important to a correct understanding of Debussy's place within what we call "Impressionism" in music. Debussy actually disliked this term when applied to his works, and perhaps with good cause. When we think of impressionism in visual art and music, we tend to think of a wash of sound and color. We might even be tempted to turn to a copious amount of pedaling (referring to any of the three pedals) to help us achieve this "washiness." Impressionistic piano music is certainly very colorful and often uses much pedal, but those colors and pedalings can and must be very precise even when we want to be carried away with great washes of sound, as happens often in Ravel, for example. Impressionism embraces a wide palette and combination of colors, but these are never blurred indiscriminately. We seek to create a "precise impression," through the precision of our interpretation.

This sense of "precise impression" is very typical of the French aesthetic. It often manifests itself in a certain reserve or distance from its subject, eschewing emotional display, and seeks an elegant refinement of execution and effect. German music is typically highly expressive, but French music is not unless the composer explicitly asks for it, as does happen often enough. At such moments we must consider whether the *expressif* quality is best expressed through a change of sound, the taking of time, or both; but it must be *thought* about and planned, especially by those of us who are not born and bred to the French aesthetic. We Americans tend to be impatient with the French world of elegant reserve, of subdued and refined emotion. Instead, we prefer to hold back very little in the name of "being real," pursuing straightforward and open honesty. Our culture is suspicious of reserve. But the beauty of entering into the music of another culture is the chance to grow in the understanding of our own, and to emerge as a greater human being. I don't believe that Debussy would call his music "reserved" in any way, but we might perceive it that way at first. The challenge is to understand and delight in its beauty on its own terms, to learn the lessons Debussy has to teach us, and not to appropriate the notes for our own purposes.

Sound and Color

Although some of the pieces contained in this volume are among the easiest pieces written by Debussy to play and learn, they should not be underestimated in terms of the technique required to play them because of the demands for precise sound production. Sound originates in the imagination and demands much of our ear (by which I mean that we must have a precise idea of the kind of sound we want), but colors are produced from the fingertips by means of touch, through the use of the damper and *una corda* pedals, and through precise voicing. One of the most notable characteristics of Debussy's music is his use of many different layers of voicing and sound, very clearly sculpted and colored through a variety of touches, often within the same hand. But even this ought not to be exaggerated.

In seeking out a colorful voicing or balance among certain layers of sound, it is useful to play the various voices of a chord or passage with two hands before trying for it with one hand. I feel it is important to get the sound in our ear first, by whatever means, before trying for its "proper" execution. If the ear demands it, the fingers and hands will find a way to produce it.

I also practice a lot without pedal to hear the honest truth about what kind of sound, color, and voicing the fingers are (or are not) producing. Then the pedals ought to be added as enhancements. Of course, we use a lot of pedal for all sorts of purposes: harmonic, melodic, coloristic, etc. Pedaling should be finely coordinated with the work of the fingers as part of the overall sound, not as the producer of sound or color.

The range of dynamics in any given piece should be strictly observed and understood in their context. Dynamics are relative to one another and to the room in which we are playing, but they are also emotional, and indicative of feeling and expression. For example, a *mezzo forte* that occurs in a piece which rarely rises above a *piano* is a dynamic of great importance (i.e., "La fille aux cheveux de lin," m. 21). But in the execution of dynamics we must not allow ourselves to be too exuberant or direct. Rather, everything is more moderate, with fine gradations of sound and color—not straight, but not straightforward, not matter of fact. An excellent example is the opening of "La cathédrale engloutie" wherein the sound by itself creates the mood because of its exploration of registers and distance, and we don't have to "add" expression or exaggerate the shape of the upward-moving lines.

Articulation

Debussy's approach to the keys was "to be one" with them—to be attached to them as extensions of our sensitive hands and fingers. This approach, combined with his famous admonition that the piano ought to be played as if it has no hammers might lead us to conclude that he desired a "mushy" or weakly articulated sound, but this is untrue. Even a cursory glance at any of his scores reveals a plethora of *staccato* notes and accents of various kinds. And then there are *portato* notes 𝄐 𝄐 𝄐, which are to be played as long *staccatos* with a *legato* shaping of the phrase (although here also, the context and character of the piece must be considered, as in "Le petit nègre," mm. 3–4). In the

case of an individual *portato* note 𝄐, the *tenuto* asks us to hold the *staccato* a little longer, functioning the same way as the slur over a group of *staccatos*. It should be noted that *staccato* sixteenths are shorter than *staccato* eights, which are in turn shorter than *staccato* quarters, and so on. Accents which lay on their side > are to be "leaned into," emphasized with a little more weight. Accents that look like a vertical wedge ∧ are played in the sharp manner we commonly associate with accents. And there are all sorts of combinations of these symbols.

When interpreting these articulation symbols in context the main considerations are length and attack. What kind of attack seems to be called for here: sharp or gentle, fast or slow, direct or caressing? Secondly, how long should the note sound? Should the eighth notes in the LH of "Le petit nègre," mm. 3–4, have the length of a sixteenth note? We should also keep in mind that the length of a note may not directly affect the speed of the attack, but it might have a direct relationship to the attack. This is for the pianist to decide. Pianists are especially guilty of neglecting the "ends" of their notes. We tend to be concerned first and foremost with the attack or "beginning" of a note, placing it exactly in time with the pulse. For those of us who are more experienced, we might be highly concerned with the sound of a note as it is singing. But the precise release of a note is just as important as the attack for crispness and clarity of expression.

As an example of the problem of grappling with Debussy's specific articulations, we may examine mm. 3–4 from another piece similar to those in this volume, "Golliwogg's cake walk" from *Children's Corner*:

We notice in that the C-flat in the first measure of this example is articulated with a wedge-accent, or played sharply. How is this different from the *staccato* wedges that articulate the final chord of the second measure? Debussy must want a much shorter note than the quarter note of the previous measure, irrespective of the dynamic. The dynamic is loud, of course, but not because of the accent. The *sforzando* takes care of that bit of information. And of course, we must be careful to make sure that the C-flat on beat 2 of the second measure is "leaned into" with a different (and gentler) articulation than the C-flat of the previous measure, thus creating a bigger surprise for us when the final chord "stamps" for our attention.

Pedaling

Debussy leaves us next to no explicit instruction in his scores of how he wanted us to use the pedals. There are some exceptions, but most often we are forced to resort to some sleuthing in order to figure out Debussy's intentions. Oftentimes Debussy will indicate his use of pedal by writing whole notes which can't be held with the fingers (such as in the opening measures of "La cathédrale engloutie"), or by the use of slur markings which tie over to nothing in particular (the final measures of "La fille aux cheveux de lin," for example). Sometimes pedaling can be used as a kind of "glue" for help in chord leaps (mm. 16 and following of "La cathédrale engloutie").

Debussy considered pedaling to be similar to breathing. I feel that the important thing about pedaling is not "when to push it down," but rather "when to release or change it, and how," much like swimmers have to be concerned with how they take breaths as they swim. Pedaling, whether using the damper pedal or the *una corda*, is perhaps the most individual of all things pianistic, very difficult to notate and reproduce from pianist to pianist or from piano to piano. Pedaling is often used to color harmonies and melodies, and sometimes for rhythmic accentuation; but there are in addition to these uses many different levels of pedaling for both the damper and the *una corda* pedals. Sensitive pianists will find themselves using quarter, half, three-quarter, and full pedals, sometimes barely touching the pedal, etc. All these uses and countless more are at our disposal, limited only by our imagination and penchant for exploration.

There are two crucial points about pedaling that should be made here. The first is very basic, but I see it in many advanced students and so I feel that I should make a statement about it: pedaling is best accomplished with the ball of the foot (that fleshy area just behind the toes) resting firmly on the end of the pedal, with the heel on the floor. A great deal of sensitivity and "oneness" with the pedal is sacrificed when students pedal with the toes or with the instep of their foot.

Secondly, great attention should be paid to the "point of engagement" of the damper pedal. We should learn to listen for the point at which the dampers begin to damp the strings as we release the damper pedal. When we become sensitive to this moment in sound, we can begin to make use of the incredible subtleties to be had by very quick and shallow half and quarter pedal changes, hovering around the "point of engagement." I have found the following exercise to be useful. It is very much like learning to drive a manual transmission car, but mercifully without the danger of stalling out:

Play any note and depress the damper pedal to hold the note while you release the key. (One could do this in reverse order, but I like hearing the change in sound from the single set of strings vibrating to the entire set of piano strings vibrating in sympathy with the struck note.) Next, slowly release the pedal until you hear that the dampers have damped the strings completely, all the while noting the change of sound as the dampers come closer to the strings. At the point where the note stops ringing, cease to release the pedal. This is the "point of engagement," as I call it, the point where the dampers are completely touching the strings. Now, release the pedal entirely. Often we are surprised at the remaining distance and how far we have to depress the pedal before the effect kicks in. The frustrating thing is that this distance is different on every piano.

Similar exercises can be developed for exploring the *una corda*—for instance, repeating a certain note with different depths of pedal. With sensitivity and knowledge of how these pedals can change the sound with subtle accuracy, we can make use of various depths of pedal for different sounds: full, deep pedal for harmonic richness, shallow pedal for coloristic affects, etc. This is all dependent on the individual's ear, and a great deal of individual experimentation by teacher and student.

Pedaling does have a connection to dynamics. The damper pedal, in particular, produces a certain volume of sound that has to be dealt with if one is after an intimate effect; we might consider using less pedal in such a case. Sometimes we can pedal through rests, because they are "articulation rests" which tell us to take our hand off the keyboard or to release a certain note for articulation purposes, not rests intended to produce silence. But other times we need to be careful to let rests speak clearly. Sometimes we must exaggerate our articulation in order to speak through the pedal. This is often the case when using *una corda*, but also we must make sure to speak clearly with our fingers while using the damper pedal. Our fingers ought not to get weak simply because our foot is coming on strong. For instance, when I use the *una corda* in combination with a *decrescendo*, it is not as a substitute for doing the *decrescendo* with my fingers, it just helps to change the quality of the sound.

Inner Voices and Fingering

Another important point to mention in connection with Debussy's music is his use of bass lines or inner voices as structural unifiers. This is typical of much of his piano music and can be very useful for grading tempo and color changes as well as establishing harmonic goals and directions. We see examples of such structural unifiers in the bass voice of the opening of "La cathédrale engloutie."

The fingering contained herein are suggestions only. Fingerings vary according to the size and flexibility of different hands, and Debussy himself believed that fingerings were intensely personal. In the preface to his *Études*, he proclaims that in this matter one is never better served than by one's own self. But just as pedaling is useful for certain colors, so I find that certain fingerings encourage certain colors from my hand, and I use it to create a true *legato*. There are far fewer possibilities for fingerings than for pedaling, so I have offered some suggestions for those who might need some workable ideas.

Notes on the Individual Pieces

These notes are by no means meant to be exhaustive in nature. Rather, they point out some of the specific technical and musical problems found in these works. The solutions I have found, especially in regard to fingering and physical motions, are hopefully well-suited to most pianists, but of course they might have to be modified for the needs of particular students and the philosophies of their teachers.

If using this volume to introduce a student to Debussy's music in a sequential way, I would suggest that "Le petit nègre" is by far the best place to start, although even this comparatively simple piece offers tricky challenges of slurring and demands minute attention to detail. From there it is a significant step up to "Clair de lune," which requires well developed *arpeggio* technique and will present the student with coloristic challenges and necessities for supple finger substitution, to say nothing of the maturity required to capture the special atmosphere. "La fille aux cheveux de lin" would be next, owing to more sophisticated pedaling challenges and the same need for supple finger substitution, but at a faster tempo than "Clair de Lune." Each "Arabesque" presents

different challenges: No. 2 is slightly easier in my experience, although a faster piece and more flashy. "La cathédrale engloutie" demands a well-developed hand, large enough to address many awkward chords with some attempt at voicing, and an excellent throwing technique in order to navigate the leaps between several layers of sound in the left hand. I save the "Rêverie" for last simply because it is truly awkward to play, requiring a deftness of coordination between the hands that is quite athletic and sophisticated.

Debussy's music was catalogued in 1977 by a French musicologist named François Lesure, who arranged Debussy's music into a roughly chronological order. We therefore identify his compositions with an "L." number; for example, "Le petit nègre," L. 114.

Le petit nègre, L. 114

Debussy composed this tiny teaching piece for Theodore Lack's 1909 *Méthode de piano*. It recalls in miniature the energy and exuberance of its more famous cousin, "Golliwogg's cake walk," from the *Children's Corner* (composed 1906–1908). The cake walk is a dance that originated in the United States during the time of slavery, involving many wildly exaggerated gestures and dance steps. Winners of cake walk competitions would be given a cake, hence the name of the dance. The style of music associated with cake walks became rapidly assimilated into ragtime, itself a genre wildly popular among the European leisure class in the early 1900s. Debussy was an admirer and wrote several pieces in this style recalling both the vaudeville shows he had seen as well as the performers themselves. "Le petit nègre" is one of them. Its title stirred social concerns when first published, and consequently was published in English (for French audiences) as "The Little Nigar." Debussy's original French title perhaps conveys a better feeling for the admiration he felt for this music and its performers.

A later edition of this piece lengthens the work by repeating its second half (mm. 22 on); I feel this is unnecessary, and much prefer the original form.

m. 1: "Allegro giusto" is a "just" or very steady Allegro, not necessarily to be played with "gusto" or too fast. Be sure that the opening tempo is appropriate for the "*a tempo*" in m. 22. In addition, be sure to play the end of the first slur with a short release, so the G does not connect to the following sixteenth-note E. The slurrings (or lack thereof) for this measure and all those following should be observed exactly: the E which finishes beat one is to be played short and on its own. The two *staccato* eighth notes that are slurred on the second beat are not to be understood as "*portamento*"; rather, the slur simply indicates that the second *staccato* eighth note is to be tapered away and played less than the first.

m. 3: Note the different slurring of the RH. It is tricky, but important, to avoid incorrect slurring!

mm. 3–4: The slur over the *staccatos* in the LH refers only to phrase shape, not as a modifier to the *staccato* articulation. Be sure to bring out the top voice of the thirds.

m. 4: Note the abundance of articulation on the RH half note! It is important to remember that it is still a half note, to be held at least as long as the first beat before being released in a *staccato* fashion.

m. 9 and following: The second eighth note in each of the LH broken octaves is less important rhythmically and should be played softer; LH should bounce over right, without rushing. Technically, this can be accomplished with the same two-note slur technique we use for the LH slurs in m. 8: drop with your wrist on the first note and release out of the second, in a single motion (double drop).

mm. 13–15: The *crescendo molto* should not preclude our being careful to shape the slurs well. Note the accents that mark the downbeats, and the various articulations and slurrings of the second beats of each measure.

m. 16: A touch of pedal to color the quarter note after the attack would be welcome, and the first need for pedal in the piece thus far.

mm. 16–20: I like to color each eighth-note pickup a little differently, perhaps each one less and more gentle than the last. The pickups swing to the following B-flats, each of which can also be colored differently.

mm. 22–25 and similar: I suggest lightly voicing the RH over the LH; pedal can be used to color and provide resonance to the RH chords which are played beneath the melody. Be carefully to cleanly change the pedal on each melody note. These chords are easily executed by understanding them as the second half of a two-note slur or double drop. This allows more freedom for a true *legato* in the RH melody. We must strive to really connect and play through each RH melody quarter note in m. 24, for example. The chords can be lightly released, but be sure to resolve the F in the last RH chord of m. 24 to the E in the following measure.

m. 26: Both hands must throw to the G with the wrists, and this is a perfect place for pedal to cover over the resulting hiccup in sound.

mm. 28–29: These *staccato* chords are to be played "up," without pedal.

m. 39: Play the LH notes with a fast attack (per the accent), but hold them for their full value (per the *tenuto*).

m. 54: These chords are to be played with a sharp and upward attack, but perhaps also with pedal for rhythmic effect.

La fille aux cheveux de lin
from *Préludes,* Première Livre, L. 117, No. 8

"The girl with the flaxen hair" appears as No. 8 in Debussy's first volume of *Préludes*, written in 1910. It is inspired, perhaps, by a poem of the same name published by Charles-Marie-René Leconte de Lisle in 1852. I say "perhaps" because in all proper editions of Debussy's preludes, the title always appears at the end of each, implying that the title is suggested by the music, not the other way around. We ought not to feel that this piece is a musical adaptation of the poem, but rather that the prelude reminds us of the poem.

The poem describes a lovely girl with golden hair, singing among blossoming lucerne-grass in the bright and fresh early morning, with cherry-red lips that invite some serious kissing. The poet describes his feelings for her and asks if they can chat pleasantly together—but begs her to say neither yes nor no; he will understand her better simply from her looking at him. A refrain runs throughout the poem: "Love, in the bright sun of summer, sang with the lark." Armed with this information, we have ample material for our imagination to draw the parallels between musical imagery and feeling and that of the original poem.

m. 1: The metronome marking seems to be Debussy's. We can use whatever fingering we wish for the first note, as long as we achieve a very light and airy (but projecting) color and sound; something gentle, with a brush of the key, without aggression or force (*sans rigueur*). However, a subsequent finger-substitution to 5 is recommended in order to facilitate the following notes, which ought to be "tucked into" the overall gesture and shape as if they are unaccented syllables in a word.

m. 3: Slide the fifth finger in the RH for the best *legato* sound possible; also in m. 10.

m. 4: We should release the end of the slur in the RH so that a new phrase begins in the following measure. Catching it with the pedal will avoid an awkward hiccup, without destroying the integrity of the phrasing. The same can be done mm. 7 and 8.

m. 6: Be sure to hold the B-flat in the RH chord on the second beat for its full value, even if we must release all notes of the chords underneath. This will help with the *legato*, which ought to be truly *cantabile* in the top voice throughout this phrase. The LH chord on beat three is difficult to place well; I suggest breaking in half, treating the bottom perfect fifth as a grace-note chord to the upper third, which should be played simultaneously with the RH chord. We must be careful to voice this chord with a strong melody note, but soft lower notes. Otherwise, the *piano* dynamic in the next measure is impossible to achieve.

m. 8: Be sure to voice the F-flat in the bass very clearly for harmonic color.

mm. 10–11: We must strive for very gentle and clear pedaling, in conjunction with a very good knowledge of which notes our fingers are holding! (Also in mm. 19–20). The "railroad tracks" at the end of the "*cedez*" marking do not indicate a lift between the melody notes, but simply mark the end of the "*cedez*." The melody should proceed (despite the rolled chord) with as little interruption as possible.

m. 13: The *piano* dynamic marking is for the accompanying chord only; the melody notes must be kept very clear. (Also in m. 16). The pedaling on the downbeat of this measure poses a particular problem: depending on the acoustic and piano (and pianist), one could change very clearly on the last eighth note of m. 12 (while holding the G-flat in the bass with the LH). Or, one could try for a half-pedal effect on the several eighth notes leading up to the downbeat of m. 13, and half-pedaling the downbeat itself. I recommend this latter technique for m. 35 into m. 36.

m. 14: As *legato* as possible in all voices, and without "sitting down" on the dotted eighth notes. (Also in mm. 33–34).

m. 15: I favor changing the pedal with the last sixteenth note of the measure, *after* which I place the LH grace note. This requires a little lengthening of the final sixteenth of m. 15; Debussy does break the slur between measures.

m. 17: Be sure to lift very gently at the end of this measure to start a new phrase in the following measure.

mm. 19–20: Be sure to listen carefully for the harmonic resolutions implied by the chords on the third beat of each measure. On the third beat of m. 20, the LH finger substitutions are rapid: the chord is played by the first, second (tied over from the previous 16th note) and fifth fingers, with 2 switching to 3 and the thumb to 2 in rapid succession thereafter.

m. 21: The *mezzo forte* is the loudest dynamic in the piece, and should be played with good feeling, but it is still only *mezzo forte*! We must grade our *crescendos* very carefully.

m. 22: The *staccato* in the RH is not meant to be short, but rather an ardent reminder that the slur is to be released so that the next chord (on the "and" of the second beat) should be played with particular emphasis of feeling. It is answered by a gentler harmonic zephyr in measure 23.

mm. 24–27: These measures are played without heaviness and without weight. At least one voice in each hand can be *legato* from chord to chord, and that makes it all sound *legato*. The bass should be played with particular attention to richness without heaviness. The *una corda* is definitely a possibility here. Be sure to highlight the beautiful relationship between the last two chords of m. 25 and the last two chords of m. 27.

mm. 30–31: Be sure to voice the alto line very carefully, from the LH thumb in m. 30 to the second finger of the RH on the downbeat of m. 31.

mm. 37–38: The rests in the LH and RH respectively are what I call "articulation" rests—not meant for silence, but simply as a result of releasing the quarter notes on the downbeats. The pedal should be held from m. 36 to the end.

La cathédrale engloutie
from *Préludes*, Première Livre, L. 117, No. 10

The legend of the sunken city of Ys, said to be located off the coast of Brittany in France, was kept alive in Breton folklore for centuries before receiving wider attention through various literary, artistic, and operatic expositions in the mid 1800s. Ys was destroyed through wanton human pride (according to many legends) as judgment for the sins of its people. Many place its location in the present-day Douarnenez Bay. Legend tells that you can hear the bells of the sunken cathedral on calm days. Debussy seems to be working from a version of the story which allows the cathedral itself to rise from the water periodically, achieving some of its lost grandeur, before slowly receding into the ocean once more.

The imagery of a sunken cathedral pervades this prelude in all ways, making it perhaps more of a piece of program music or representational music than many of the others in both volumes of *Préludes*. One hears unmistakably the bells, the chants of priests and monks, the very acoustics of a cathedral achieved through incredibly long pedalings and massive sonorities. E. Robert Schmitz draws attention to the similar shaping of the phrasing to arches that might be found in a typical cathedral. Because of these attributes, "La cathédrale engloutie" can provide a fascinating study in scene painting at the piano.

m. 1: The metronome marking is mine. In the opening of this prelude, it is useful to sit up very straight and allow your fingers to come out of the keys. There ought to be some firmness in the fingers, but gentleness and suppleness at the fingertip. The first chord produces a ping, within which we color the sonorities of the rising quarter-note chords, rising like bubbles in one arm gesture, articulated like very long *staccatos*. Remember your meter, playing in a calm six beats per measure; not too fast. Pedaling should follow the tied notes in the LH (i.e., one pedal for two measures).

m. 2: Be sure to make a distinction between the *staccato* sonorities and the *tenuto* on the fifth beat; the *tenuto*, however, should be softest.

mm. 1–16: Without a true *crescendo*, be sure to follow the descending bass line from G all the way down to B in m. 16. This helps to tie the architecture together and grade your harmonic colors.

m. 5: There should be a feeling of arrival at the E's on beat 2, at which point we start to voice the top note with a gentle "ping." The melody of the following measures, however, weaves over and under this bell-like E, so a different sonority must be reserved for that melodic line, with careful distinctions of voicing.

m. 7: Much has been written about the intentions of Debussy at this point in the prelude, specifically about the tradition of doubling the time. What finally convinced me about this was the fact that pianists and musicians who knew Debussy and have left recordings, or who have orchestrated the piece with Debussy's blessing, doubled the tempo. Whether the time is doubled exactly or flows more freely (after the manner of Gregorian Chant) is a matter of artistic interpretation. In any case, the melody should be fluid like plainchant.

m. 13: There ought to be a little freedom here as the bell swings back and forth, and we resume the initial tempo.

mm. 14–15: Be sure to feel one long line throughout the RH chords. Although Debussy writes *sans nuances*, be sure to shape the swinging bells in the LH gently. Throwing to the bass chord on the downbeat of m. 15 ought to be done as delicately as with a handkerchief, being sure to resolve beautifully to the downbeat of m. 16.

mm. 16 and following: Be sure to voice the fifth finger in the RH chords. It is useful to lead with the wrist as we navigate these chordal arches. The damper pedal should be released on the downbeats that require a rest in the bass line (m. 17, etc.). The *una corda* should have been depressed since the beginning of the prelude, but beginning in m. 16 or so, we can very gradually release it so as to arrive by m. 21 at a full *tre corde* sound.

mm. 19–21: Don't change the pedal in mm. 19 and 21, but keep the harmonic color uninterrupted. Clarity can be achieved through voicing. I would change the pedal on the downbeat of m. 21, however. The *marqué* gestures ought to be thrown to and away from with bravery and freedom in the arm, getting as many notes as possible in one gesture.

mm. 22 and following: Bright sound can be achieved with firm fingertips and supple wrist and arm. The LH should follow the slurs in sweeping three-note gestures, avoiding verticality by using the wrist. The RH follows the same shapes in mm. 25–26.

mm. 25–27: Because of various pianos and acoustics, we might find ourselves needing to change pedal on each beat in the bass. This might be required for clarity, but we should not sacrifice resonance and a constantly expanding sonority. Longer pedals (at least every two beats) would be preferable.

m. 28: The bass C is played an octave below what is written, several fingers in unison, for a grand gong-like effect (not harsh, but "out" of the key). The *sff* G in the RH of the measure preceding this ought to be quite sharp so we can hear the dominant resolve to the tonic.

mm. 28–41: It is very effective to use one pedal (don't change at all) throughout these measures, perhaps with small half-changes on each half note in m. 41. In order to achieve a sonority "without harshness" (*dureté*), be sure to follow through your full chords with your arm, rising with the wrists out of each chord and floating to the next, albeit with full weight behind each sound. And we must take care to shape the phrases well, although we remain *fortissimo* for the duration of this section.

mm. 42–45: The dotted whole notes are to be played with more resonance than the coloristic chords which sound on the second beats. We can gradually depress the *una corda* throughout these measures. The color chords, however, should be voiced towards the outsides of the hands. This becomes important in m. 46, where the A-flat turns into a G-sharp. By gently voicing the top of the G-sharp octave (instead of the bottom A-flat, as in previous measures), we can draw attention to this color change.

mm. 47 and following: Be sure to shape the line well despite the slow tempo. Because it is a single monk, we could play without pedal for four measures until he is joined by more in measure 51. An unpedaled sound will achieve the concentration Debussy asks for. Be sure to hold the bass G-sharp while observing the LH rests in m. 49.

mm. 55–60: Note the LH arch shapes, voicing the thumb for clarity. By m. 57 we should have fully released the *una corda*.

mm. 59–62: These chords in both hands feel awkward to play; therefore, it is necessary to collect your hand after playing each and to relax the arms and wrists as much as possible as you float from chord to chord. In m. 60, be sure to swing with the LH arm all the way to the downbeat of m. 61, taking as part of that motion the chords and octaves on the fifth beat.

mm. 62–66: Pedal each chord progressively adding *una corda* to help with the *diminuendo* and achieving a deepening purple sunset (or something like that). Great attention should be payed to the color of *each* note in the harmonies.

m. 68–70: The bells on the downbeats ought to be slightly more sonorous than the C-natural bells, although the C-natural in m. 69 needs to have enough sound to continue through its syncopated entrance into the continuous ringing of m. 70 and following. The switch of hands in m. 71 must be seamless.

m. 72 and following: It is not important that every note in the LH speak clearly, but it is important that every note "be there" in the haze and that the *ostinato* is shaped well. If one voices well, one doesn't need to change pedal at all from m. 69 until m. 84. Long pedals are also welcome after the change at m. 84; perhaps only half pedals on the downbeats of mm. 85–87, after which we allow the sound to die away without pedal change. Be sure to keep fairly strictly in time; Debussy has written out the *rallentando* he wants. Although we can let the sound ring a little

longer than the rests in the final measure might indicate, we should be sure to listen to the silence after we release the pedal. It is important enough to Debussy to have been notated.

Deux Arabesques, L. 66

These short pieces date from early in Debussy's life and career. They were composed between 1888 and 1891, influenced by the flowing, intertwining designs that Debussy so admired in graphic art (arabesques feature heavily in Arabic or Moorish decoration, and found their way into the works of one of Debussy's favorite painters, Jean-Antoine Watteau) as well as in the Baroque music of J.S. Bach and his contemporaries. Above all, Debussy admired the way that a line (musical or graphic) could be shaped to the movements and laws of nature. This admiration brought to these pieces their flowing, graceful natures, whether gracious (No. 1) or capricious (No. 2). Although not representative of the greatness of his later compositions, these two pieces nevertheless have become exceedingly popular and are often the first encounter for many people with Debussy's music.

Première Arabesque

m. 1: The metronome indication is mine, although this music calls for a flexible tempo and pulse and should by no means be metronomic. All of our *rallentandos* and expressive time-taking, however, should be classically proportioned, eschewing a romantic tendency toward exaggeration.

mm. 1–5 and similar: Since these are arpeggiated chords, the fingers can fill out the sound by using finger *legato* and prolonging the sound of each note, shaping the *arpeggios* into true chords. This allows for a greater or lesser use of pedal, as dictated by the piano and the acoustic, although changing every half measure is a good starting point. We must be careful, however, not to accent the G-sharp on the third beat of m. 1 or the E on the third beat of m. 2 as if they are melody notes (as in mm. 17–18). Be sure to shape the LH half notes as a beautiful line leading to the dominant in m. 5.

m. 5: I would use one pedal for the whole measure to prolong the dominant bass in our ear. There are no *tenutos* over the final G-sharp and F-sharp in the RH of this measure as there are in the analogous m. 75. Therefore, this *ritardando* needs to be played more gently, taking less time.

m. 6 and following: The E in the bass ought to be warm and given a gently different harmonic color than the rest of the *arpeggio*; an imaginative use of varying levels of *una corda* can be helpful here as well as a slow change of the damper pedal whenever a change occurs. The LH makes use of a throwing motion to negotiate the *arpeggio*, but avoid any kind of real *crescendo*; it should remain a beautifully shaped accompaniment that does not challenge the RH melody. The RH gesture ought to be like a gentle and trickling waterfall that descends without rushing into a richly ornamented ascending melodic scale in mm. 10 and following. Be careful not to allow false accents in the long melodic line.

mm. 13–14: The LH can employ a rolling motion from the wrist to help with shaping these arpeggiated chords. Every note should have its own color, as if voicing individual notes in a chord, paying close attention to how the bass notes climb the stairs and outline the harmony in their own right. Since we are playing only one note at a time, there is no need to try to cover the entire chord with an outstretched hand; allow the hand to collect as it rolls through each arpeggio.

mm. 19 and following: The LH wrist continues to roll and the hand to collect as we trace the *arpeggio* with good attention paid to the harmonic resolutions of the bass notes (F-double sharp on the first beat to the G-sharp on the third, etc.) as well as a sensitive thumb, which can hint at a beautiful descending scalar line of its own. Be generous, giving full value and a *cantabile* sound to the straight eighth-note duples in the RH over the triplets in the LH (beats 3 and 4 of m. 20, for example) whenever Debussy employs them.

m. 26 and following: The triplet accompaniment in the lower fingers of the RH should murmur underneath the whole-note melody, which ought not to lose too much of our attention as we shape the melodic phrase over several measures.

mm. 31 and 33: These measures can be played with one pedal, but the transitions from hand to hand must be smoothed out by practicing without pedal.

m. 32: The LH takes the downbeat E, in order to continue the descending *legato* line; the same fingering is useful at the downbeat of m. 34 to preserve the tied notes in the RH.

mm. 34–37: This can be an awkward passage until we realize that the RH fifth finger is simply following an E-major scale. For greater security, practice the fifth finger by itself, and then the triplets underneath by themselves (with the fingering that you would use when playing all the notes together in the RH). We can drop

the wrist and roll out of each triplet gesture in the RH, employing the same fingering for each, which minimizes complications. Also, it is important to understand the LH as outlining a single dominant seventh arpeggio, not a series of unrelated notes.

m. 38: Use the rest in the LH as an opportunity to change the pedal slowly, not abruptly. The E in the RH on the downbeat must be played with enough sound to still be heard as the start of the new melody in m. 39.

m. 39 and following: The tempo *rubato* can make use of a clearer sound to help delineate the new section. Hear how the color changes under the tied E (from m. 38) as we change harmony on the downbeat; although we strive to keep the melody legato, because we are using pedal, we can release each of the accompanying chords in this measure and the ones following. When releasing chords, however, we must take care to precisely release all the notes together so we don't inadvertently cause messiness due to ragged releases either between hands or within a single hand. Remember that the damper pedal magnifies everything our fingers are doing well—or not doing well.

mm. 41–42: We release the E on the "and" of the first beat in the RH as if it were the second note of a two-note slur in order to throw to the chord on the second beat. But this E should not be thrown away like a slur ending, but rather retained as part of the melodic line. We must voice the chords carefully so that the top voice sings out gently. The fingering in these measures and those following presumes adult-sized hands.

mm. 47–48: Release each slur in the RH so you can begin the new wrist gesture easily, rolling from your thumb through the triplets. Also note that the slurring for the LH is contrary to the RH phrasing; this adds more "swirl" to the piece. Be sure to change the pedal promptly on the downbeat of m. 48.

m. 49: The *forte* dynamic is not for every note, but rather for the arrival of the melody note on the second beat; be careful not to whack it, and to voice and shape the other chords for the relaxing of your phrase into the end of m. 50. In addition, we must be careful to be *legato* with our fingers from the F-sharp that finishes the first-beat triplet to the A which arrives on the second beat, regardless of whether we employ the pedal here or not. The same care needs to be taken in mm. 53–54, although the *forte* arrival in m. 54 should be greater than in m. 53. Note as well that the LH in these measures differs from m. 49 in that there is no slur; the chords on beat 3 are consequently more emphatic.

m. 62: Even though there is a *crescendo*, the LH slur should be shaped well, with no accent on the last beat. In the following *risoluto*, be careful to follow through each chord with supple wrists to avoid a hard sound.

mm. 67–68: Be sure to voice the LH thirds well, with the top note gently stressed.

m. 70: For the LH finger substitution, I would switch to the thumb on the G-sharp first, and afterwards to the third finger on the E.

mm. 89 and following: Be sure to fit the triplet *arpeggio* in the LH *into* the sound of the half notes on every half measure; they should be harmonic color. We also need to carefully shape the "thumb line" in the RH of these measures.

mm. 95–99: Be sure to hear and shape the whole-note line like a *legato* scale. We should hold the pedal through mm. 95 and 96, this is the reason for the double whole note (downbeat of m. 95) and the lack of LH rests in m. 96.

mm. 103–105: The tempo from here to the end of the piece can be released. The LH should be as *legato* as possible within each measure, shaped with a tiny *decrescendo* over the length of the slur. The first note of each of the RH gestures can form a gentle echoing melody as it rises through the successive registers. Be sure to hide the thumb, as if releasing a two-note slur.

m. 107: This final note is very typical of early Debussy. It does not belong to the preceding phrase, but is rather a sort of "gentle period" or other such punctuation mark to finish the piece.

Deuxième Arabesque

m. 1 and similar: The metronome indication is mine. The arabesque figure is a great pleasure to play if one allows the fingers to be free (but articulate), tossed through each gesture with a double drop like one uses in two-note slurs. The release of each gesture can easily propel us to the following one.

mm. 1–4: The harmonic rhythm is very slow, and each LH chord should be colored differently. Keep the bass line *legato*, minimizing the need for pedal which would obscure RH clarity; small touches of pedal throughout these measures (and the entire piece) will warm up the sound.

m. 5 and similar: The perfect fifth on the fourth beat of the LH should be less loud, resolving from the chord on the downbeat. Similarly, in m. 7 the bass must be well shaped with the B on the downbeat resolving to the C on the second beat, etc.

mm. 6–8 and similar: When rolling the LH chords fast, it is important not to try to cover the entire chord, but rather to allow the hand to collect as you roll up the chord. The top note (thumb) should arrive with the top note of the RH. The exception to this might be the downbeats of mm. 5, 6, 9, etc., where, if the hand is sufficiently large, we should hold the chord in its entirety and voice the thumb.

m. 13: Although not marked as such, I would play the LH *molto staccato*.

m. 14: The LH eighth notes on beat two should be played *staccato* as well. Take care to hold and gently voice the half-note A on the downbeat, and hear its resolution to the final D of the measure.

mm. 15–16 and following: The left-hand harmonies should be well shaped. I prefer to resolve the downbeat of m. 16 from the perfect fifth of the previous measure with the G octave (and its subsequent chord) as a further resolution. This shaping must be independent of the RH dynamic shaping.

m. 19: Please note that the melody is found in the LH. The slurs in the RH should be well shaped over the next few measures.

m. 27: A tiny bit of pedal on the rolled chord would be very sweetly appropriate. The roll itself needn't be too fast. It should be delicate enough to taste the A-sharp which defines the augmented chord.

m. 29 and similar: The RH *staccato* should be firm but melodic. Note that in m. 31, the LH F-sharp which forms the top voice of the chord on the third beat is NOT part of the melody. Careful voicing must be used to ensure that we hear the rest as an interruption.

mm. 38–41: We should feel free to lift both hands every other beat as we shift (expand) hand positions.

mm. 46–49: The quarter notes in the RH thumb should also be played *staccato*. The thumbs which take two notes simultaneously in the LH of mm. 47–48 are to accommodate smaller hands.

m. 49: The last beat in the LH should be played with warm gentleness. It begins a beautiful countermelody, but the principal melody beginning in the RH of m. 50 should be louder.

mm. 56–57: Both hands should be completely *legato*, contrasting mm. 52–53.

mm. 58–61: Long pedals throughout these measures are very effective.

m. 72–73 and similar: Be sure to use one wrist/arm gesture to accomplish the overall slur of the LH half-notes (releasing the third beat of m. 73).

m. 75: Even though we are using pedal, the articulation should sound different from measure 73.

mm. 76–82: It is effective to play mm.76–79 completely dry, starting to add color pedals for the two-note slurs in mm. 80 and 81, before employing very long pedals beginning in m. 82. (A similar progression of adding pedal could be followed mm. 90–100). I would change the pedal on the third beat of m. 83 and the subsequent downbeat of m. 84, but then hold the pedal for two measures to prolong the harmonic color. Similar pedaling might be applied to mm. 86–89.

mm. 98–99: Even though we are using pedal, try to be *legato* in the bass line of the LH.

Rêverie, L. 68

In 1891, Debussy found himself in want of funds. Accordingly, he collected some previously-composed shorter pieces, as well as dashing off several new ones, and sold them in various bundles to the publisher Antoine Choudens for what they might bring. The "Rêverie" (L. 68), a mazurka (L. 67), a ballade (L. 70), and several other works were among these. Debussy's later opinion of the "Rêverie" was very low. Although it is filled with some very exquisite ideas and harmonic subtleties, a very brief reading will present a possible reason for Debussy's distaste: it is less well-worked out pianistically than most of his later works, and consequently awkward to play. Its conclusion is also rather trite, as if Debussy could not find a more suitable closing in the short time he had, and simply and abruptly wrapped up the piece.

Be this as it may, the "Rêverie" is deservedly beloved for its good qualities, and can be athletically very fun as well. The trick is to be as smooth and unruffled as possible while accomplishing quite amazing feats of dexterity. It is also a challenge to find the right frame of mind for its performance: a sort of gentle and pleasant distraction, here and there tinged by a melancholy desire, and briefly, a gently determined optimism.

mm. 1–10: The tempo ought to flow out in order to enable a very long line from the beginning; mm. 1–10 form a complete and unbroken thought. It is worth noting that after the initial downbeat, we don't experience a settled arrival on the downbeat until we achieve the tonic key in m. 9—another circumstance which should keep the wind in our sails as we flow through the first ten measures. We should also be careful not to over-express the melodic shapes in this long line—the expression can come from the color of the sound, and the gentle contours of the melody.

m. 11: *Meno piano* means "less piano"—louder!

mm. 11 and following: We need to employ gentle throws to navigate these LH *arpeggios*: from the thumb to the fifth finger in the first two beats of m. 11, to the fifth finger on beat 3 of m. 12, back down to the fifth finger on the downbeat of m. 13, etc. Don't try to reach, but use the wrist to get where you need to go.

m. 19 and following: I chose this fingering in the LH to keep the hand as collected and comfortable as possible since I don't believe that we need to try to cover an arpeggiated chord entirely with a stretched-out palm; we only need to play one note at a time, and glide with our wrist through the *arpeggios*. (The LH fingering in m. 24 may feel a little awkward, so I included an alternate in parentheses; I prefer my first suggestion, since it avoids placing both thumbs together on a comparatively strong beat, and risking a false accent.) Concerning the octaves in the RH, we want to try for as *legato* a line as possible; this is often accomplished by trying to keep at least one voice *legato* from octave to octave. In any case, the stationary E-flat in the RH of mm. 19–21 acts as a pivot, allowing our hand to swing freely from octave to octave, and to get as many octaves as possible into one wrist gesture (i.e., the triple drop at the beginning in m. 21). There are further stationary pivot notes in subsequent measures, and it is always vital to cultivate a supple, "collecting" hand (and flowing arm) while playing octaves, to avoid stiffness and a hard sound.

mm. 28: Be sure to hold the thumb for its full value in the RH; also in m. 30.

mm. 35 and following: It is useful to feel that the RH wrist bobs along in two big beats per measure, but we should take care that this does not affect the shaping of the LH melody. The gentle release of the wrist at the end of each "bobbing motion" is especially useful in m. 40 at which point the RH needs to release after the second beat to throw to the chord on the third beat.

m. 47: The LH should not release the C (on the "and" of two) too soon in order to create as *legato* a connection to the B-flat as possible. This is exceedingly difficult and requires a gentle throw of the hand from the wrist, combined with a gentle roll that voices the top B-flat as part of the continuing line into m. 48 (the melodic line is assumed by the RH thumb).

m. 48: The LH should take the final two eighth notes of this measure, lightly throwing from the C an octave beneath, and softly coloring the RH melody.

m. 51: In pedaling these *portamento* chords, we should strive to catch the note with the pedal while we are still touching the key before releasing our fingers. This requires a very subtle and shallow pedal technique that does not release the pedal completely past the point of its engagement (see preface). In these chords and in all the measures following, acute attention to voicing is required; a good way to practice is to play the outer voices alone, *tenuto*, and then with the inner voices played *staccato*. This balances the weight nicely in the hand. However, Debussy is not interested in a highly colored or brightly shining outer voice; his performances were more subdued, and we ought to be careful not to overdo our voicing.

m. 56: The B on the fourth beat must be played gently since it begins an inner voice, and the principal melody starts on the following downbeat.

mm. 67–68: The LH can be made to conform to a single gesture for the entire measure; mm. 69–70, however, will probably require that a single gesture be used for each half-measure in both hands. The LH melody in mm. 69–70 should be practiced on its own for voicing purposes.

mm. 76–82: The melody which passes between the hands ought to be practiced by itself until a smooth transition using consistent fingering is achieved and beautifully shaped. The hands will need to be gently thrown from gesture to gesture by the wrists.

m. 86 and following: Note the dynamic differences from the opening of the piece.

m. 95: The LH "A" which falls on the fourth beat should be played softly as an unaccented syllable; it does not belong to the LH melody that begins in m. 96.

m. 99: A tiny sigh before the downbeat of m. 100 would be appropriate.

Clair de lune
from *Suite bergamasque*, L. 75, No. 3

Surely the most well-known and arguably the best-loved of Debussy's oeuvre, "Clair de Lune" ("Moonlight") is a special piece unto its own despite its appearance as the third movement of the *Suite bergamasque*, which was written in 1890 and revised somewhat for publication in 1905. In that context, it could be understood as a kind of sarabande, especially in light of its motion to the second beats of many of the opening measures, its predominantly slow tempo, and voluptuous lines. But as a piece of musical magic, it stands with any movement of any piece in all of Debussy's output.

The best performances of "Clair de lune" are patient, loving, and attentive above all to beauty of sound and flow of rhythm. The music should enchant us, not stir us emotionally.

m. 1–14: Note that we start with a rest, which must be felt if the rhythm of the first gesture is to be executed well; subdividing the triplets in our heart from the very beginning is part of the secret to making our *rubatos* organic in the first fourteen measures or so—not so that we may be metronomically inflexible, but rather so we can feel our time organically and fluidly yet still tied to three triplets (of whatever value) per pulse. This will be important as we feel the resistance to the inner pulse in measures that include duplets (mm. 3, 13, etc.) Voicing must be carefully sculpted throughout, with a very beautiful *legato* in as many voices as possible through finger substitution.

m. 1: Be sure to feel the distance from LH A-flat to RH A-flat—the expression is in the reaching.

m. 9: Take your time through the triplet, to hear the colors of each register and feel the distance between them.

m. 10 and similar: Be careful not to accent the chords which appear on offbeats; technically and musically they should be released from the long notes which precede them.

m. 11 and following: We will hold the pedal through the entire measure, because of the dotted half note in the bass. Additionally, the last notes of each measure in the RH should be held as we change the pedal for the following downbeat.

m. 15: and following "*Rubato*" is an Italian term that originates in the word "*rubare*," which means "to steal." Stealing means that you don't give back. My understanding of this *tempo rubato* then, is to steal time and then return to tempo as if nothing ever happened. This works both ways: one could flow faster or slower, but proportions need not be mathematically evened out. What ought to be observed more carefully, in fact, is the *tenuto* articulations, for example in m. 15. When we see them, we should be fairly even and equal; when we don't see them (i.e., m. 14), we can be free. Therefore, on the downbeat of m. 15, I prefer to "feel" the E-flat octave rather than to plant it, to let the sound float up from that register to the magical chord on the second half of that beat—but outside of any tempo. It recalls the opening reach of the piece.

m. 18: The grace note is melodic and should not be played too fast. Be sure to hold the last chord in the RH as you change pedal for m. 19.

m. 19 and similar: Be sure to voice the melody in the RH and LH with softer chords inside and a fluid shape. The *crescendo* can be graded by listening to the ascent of the bass line (listening to harmonic resolutions along the way), and then the *diminuendo* shaped by its fall in mm. 25–26. Throughout, pay close attention to the presence of *tenutos* or lack thereof.

mm. 25–26: The rolled chords should be expressive and varied in tempo, not just ripped off in one speed. Personally, I don't mind a continuous roll from bottom to top, as opposed to the traditional execution of broken rolls when notated this way.

m. 27: "Un poco mosso" means "a little moving," it is true—but not too much faster! Already we are in contrast to the slowing tempo of the previous measures, by virtue of the rolling *arpeggios*.

mm. 27–29: Be careful to observe the phrasing of each measure, which should *diminuendo* and release in the RH (except in the presence of a *crescendo*, as in m. 29). The accompanimental *arpeggios* in these measures, although broken between the hands, should be carefully shaped to taper away at the end of each slur with gentle emphasis on the bass notes as we change color with each new harmony. The LH should not feel obliged to *crescendo* in tandem with the RH in m. 29; rather, all of mm. 29 and 30 should feel like the slow cresting of a particularly warm and caressing wave of water.

m. 30: I would encourage the LH thumb to pretend it is a French horn when the melodic echo starts on the second beat; a rather bronzed sound, hollow but *maestoso*, not too forceful and a little distant (but present at the same time). The RH should continue with this sound. The

orchestration of the RH starting m. 29 is left to the discretion of the performer.

m. 32: Be sure to observe the *subito piano*; this is a very typical dynamic occurrence in Debussy's music.

m. 33: The RH wrist can use the sixteenth notes to gently circle around to the next melody notes.

m. 37: It is at this point that we should start to release the *una corda*, which should have been depressed up to this moment from the start of the piece (with a possible hiatus mm. 21–25). Be sure to release the last sixteenth note of each RH group in preparation for the next gesture.

mm. 43–50: The "*calmato*" can refer also to sound, not just tempo. We can resume coloring with the *una corda* at m. 43 (perhaps not fully depressed yet). I suggest that we plan most of the *rallentando* for mm. 49–50.

m. 43: When throwing the hand to the RH chord on beat 3, take care to resolve the melody in the thumb and hold it all the way through to the end of the measure; also in m. 44. Measures 45–46 present similar challenges in the RH on beat 3 in each measure; the LH addresses these challenges in mm. 47–48.

m. 45: In beat three, the LH thumb should cross underneath the RH thumb.

mm. 51–end: This concluding section must feel airy and timeless, although for the performer it will be essential to subdivide as at the beginning of the piece.

m. 51 and similar: The *tenuto* on the third beat should be well-placed and played softly in order conserve the feeling of a "third beat," not an "equal pulse" within the measure.

m. 53: Please note the difference between the RH second beat of this measure and that of m. 3.

m. 65: Treat the duple in the LH very lightly; the melody note on the second beat is the F in the RH. The LH A-flat which crosses the RH at that moment simply shines as a color.

m. 71: As we move from sixteenths to eighth notes, we must be careful to effect a smooth transition, without bumps.

References

Dumesnil, Maurice. *How to Play and Teach Debussy*. New York: Schroeder and Gunther, Inc., 1932.

Long, Marguerite. *At the Piano with Debussy*, trl. Olive Senior-Ellis. London: J.M. Dent and Sons Ltd., 1972.

Raad, Virginia. *The Piano Sonority of Claude Debussy*. Lewiston/Queenston/Lampeter: The Edwin Mellen Press, 1994.

Schmitz, E. Robert. *The Piano Works of Claude Debussy*. New York: Dover Publications, Inc., 1966.

Audio Credits

David Lau, Recording Engineer,
Brookwood Studios

Mi-Eun Kim and Sonya Schumann,
Recording Assistants

Steinway Piano

Le petit nègre

Claude Debussy
L. 114

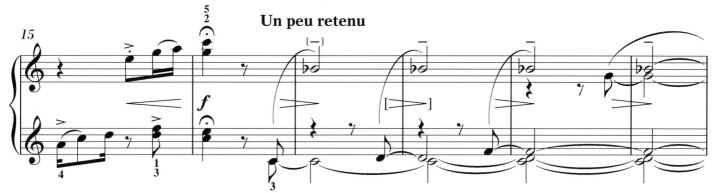

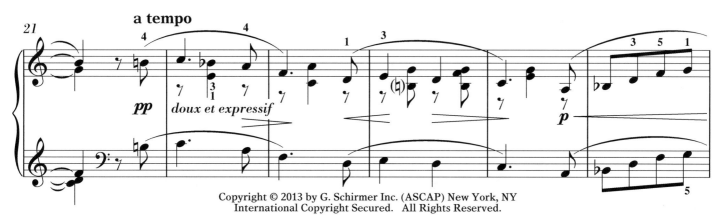

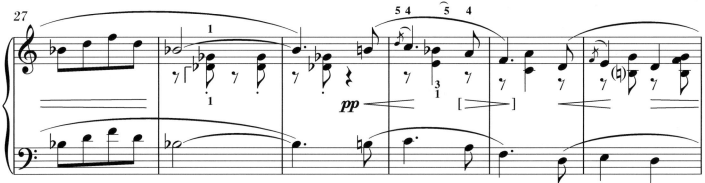

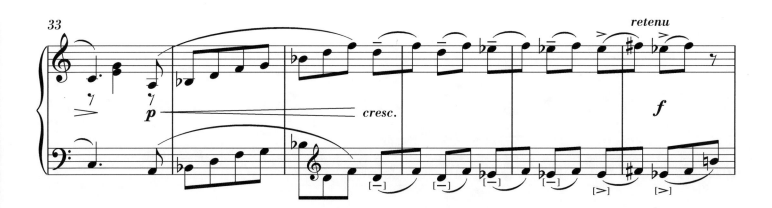

La fille aux cheveux de lin

from *Préludes*, Première Livre

Claude Debussy
L. 117, No. 8

Très calme et doucement expressif [♩ = 66]

La cathédrale engloutie

from *Préludes*, Première Livre

Claude Debussy
L. 117, No. 10

Profondément calme (Dans une brume doucement sonore) [♩ = 60]

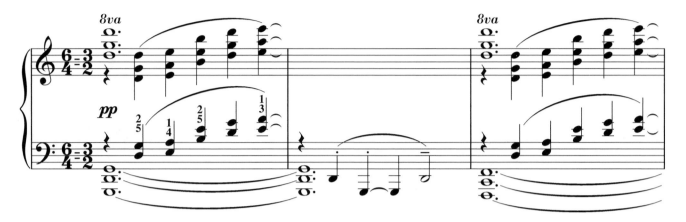

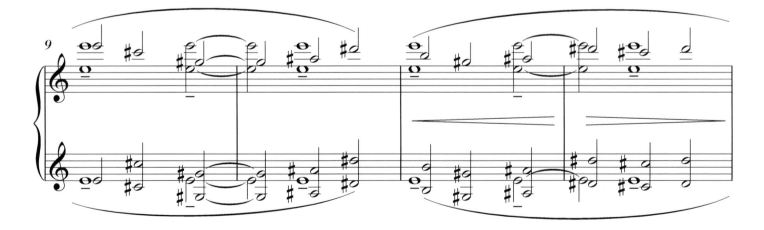

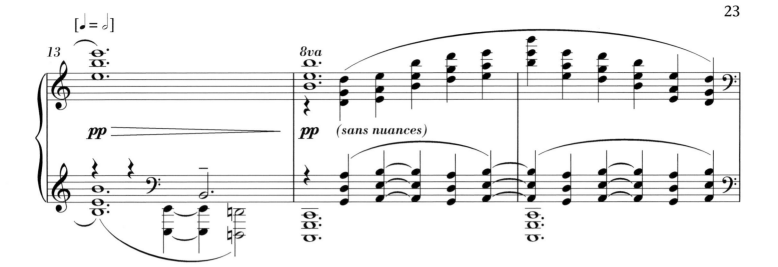

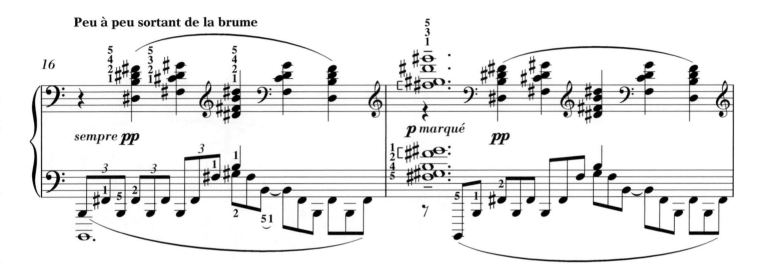

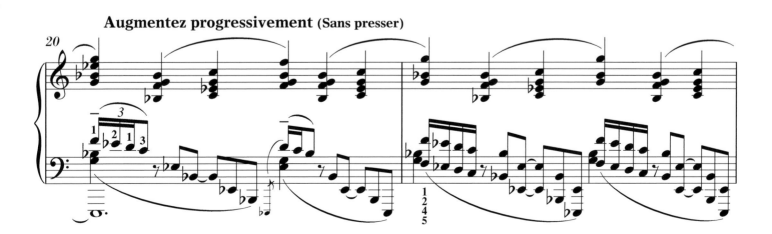

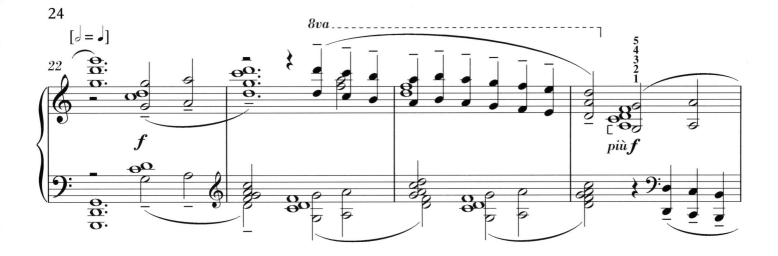

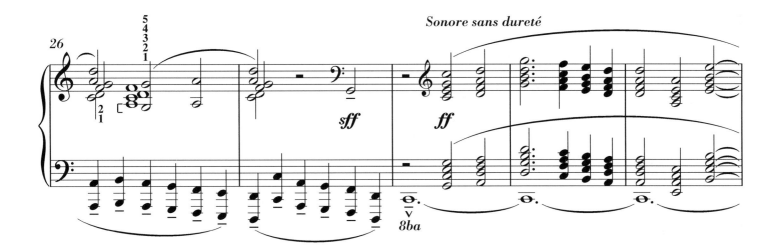

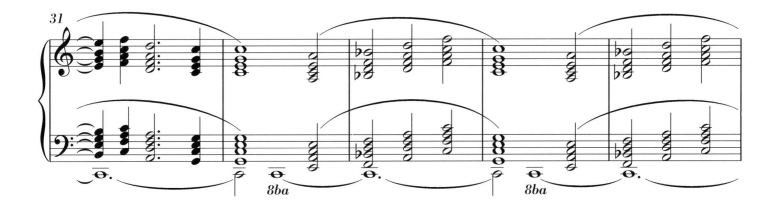

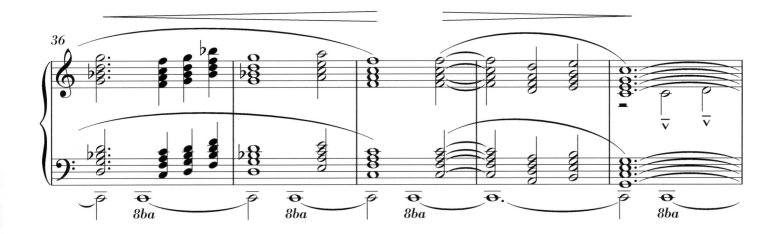

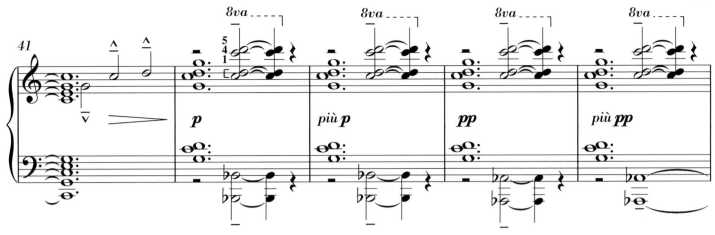

Un peu moins lent (dans une expression allant grandissant)

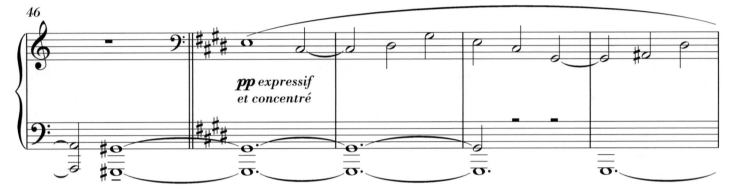

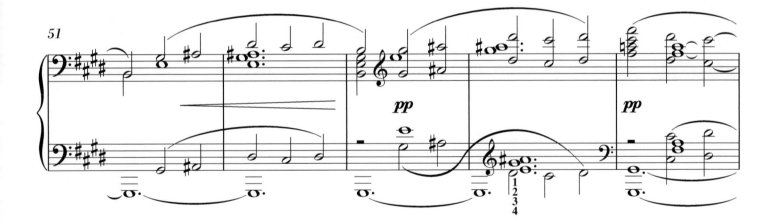

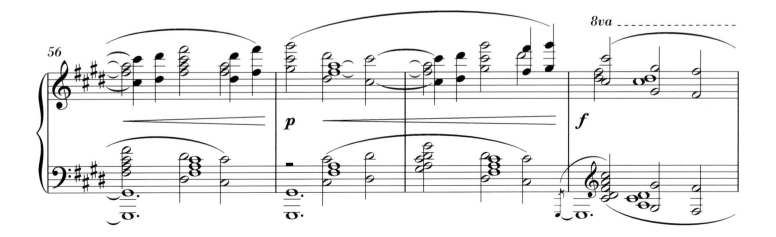

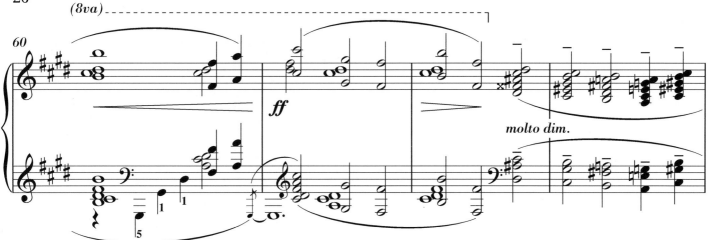

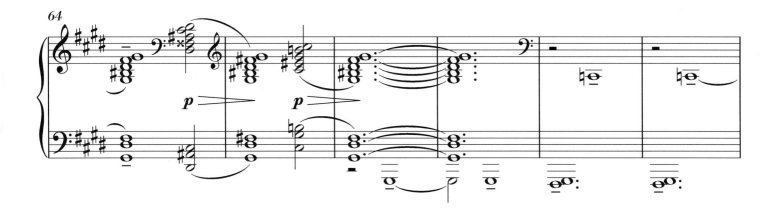

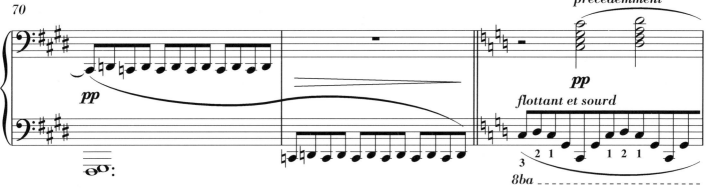

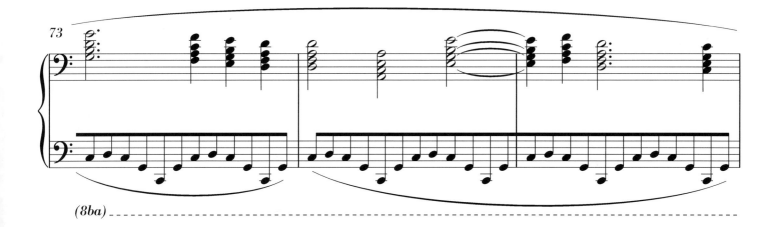

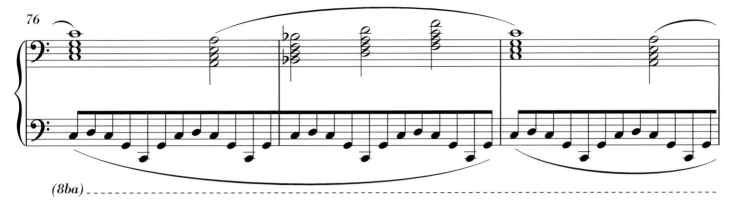

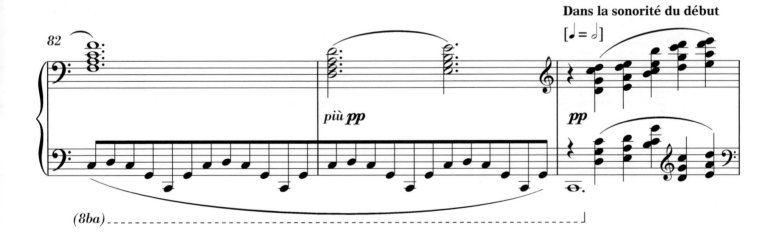

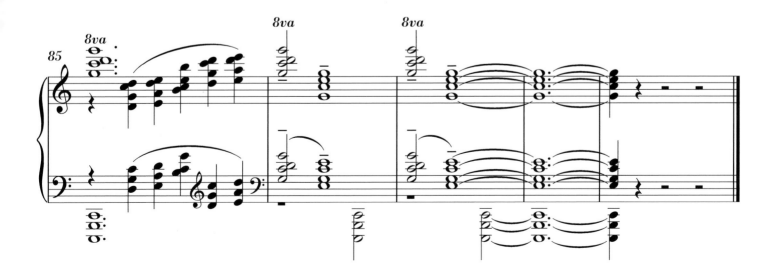

Deux Arabesques
Première Arabesque

Claude Debussy
L. 66, No. 1

Andantino con moto [♩ = 120]

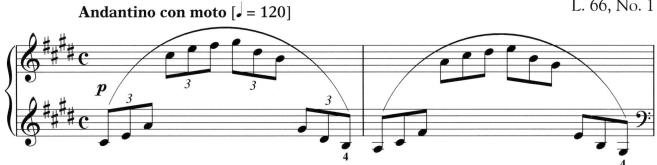

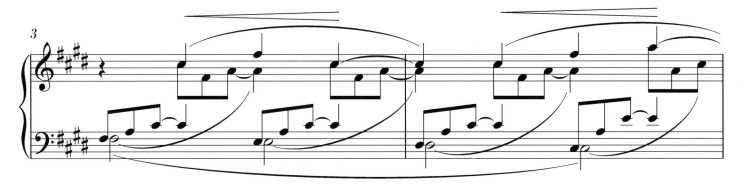

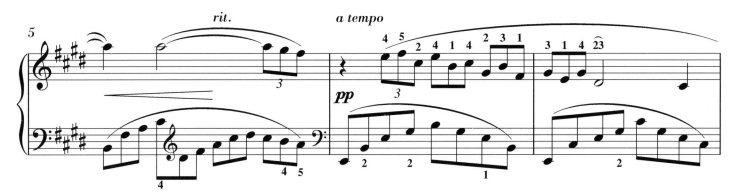

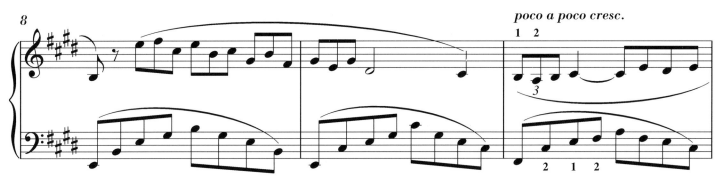

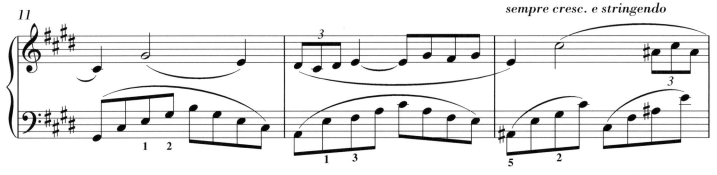

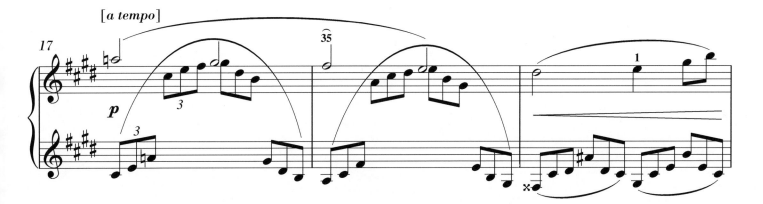

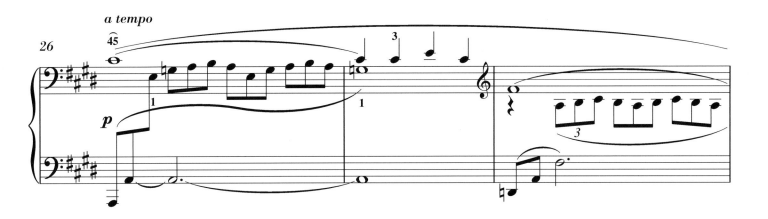

cresc. e poco mosso

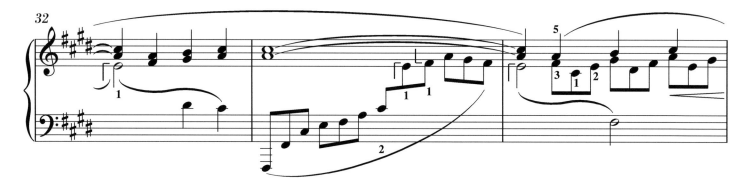

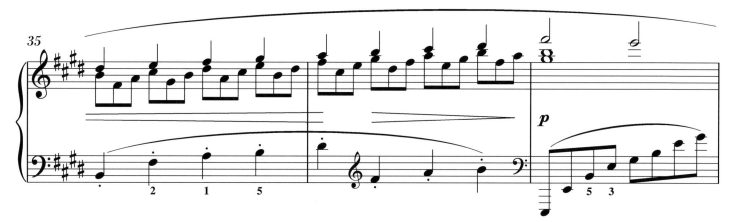

Tempo rubato (un peu moins vite)

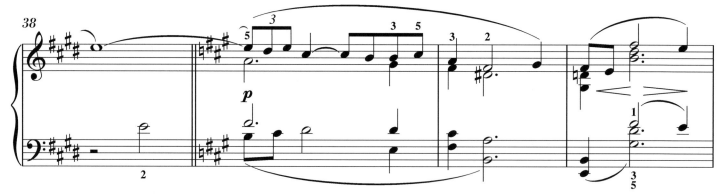

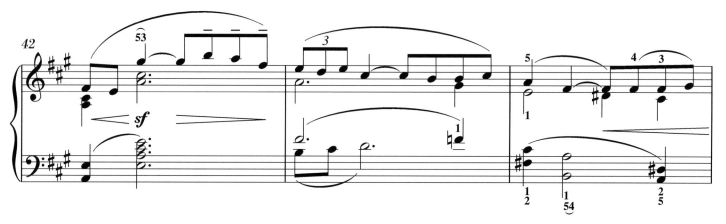

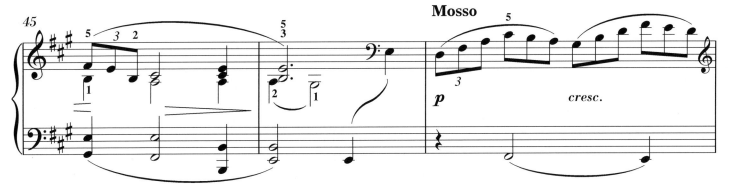

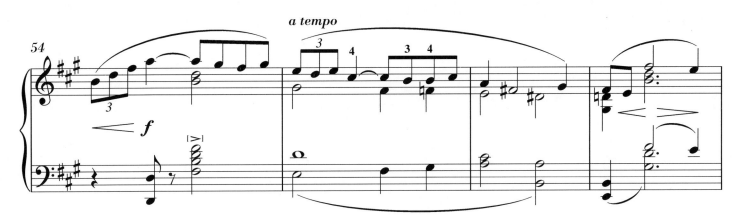

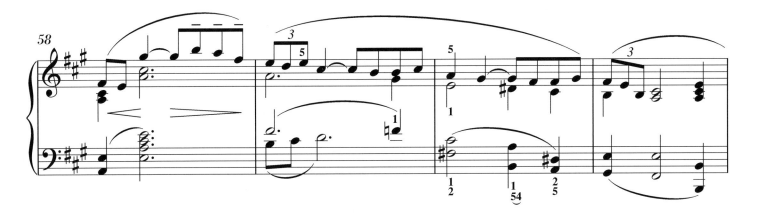

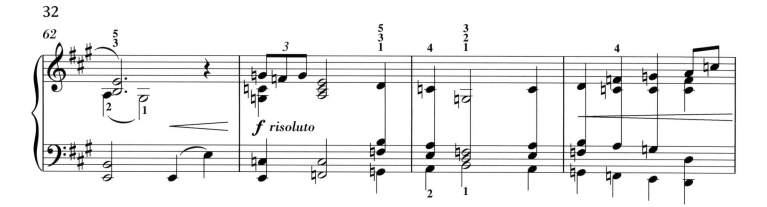

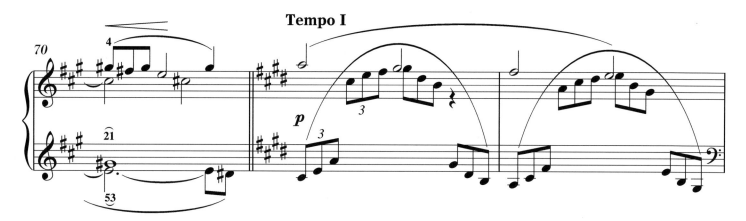

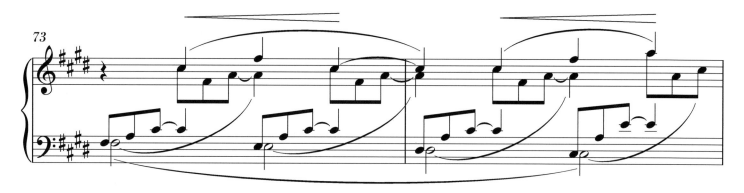

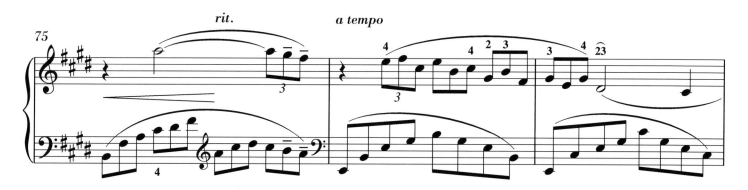

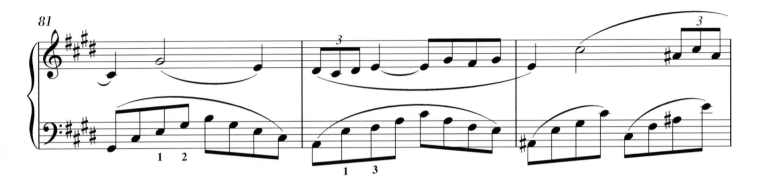

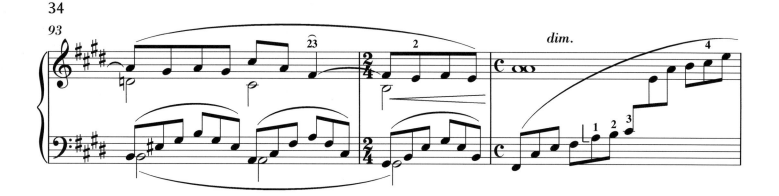

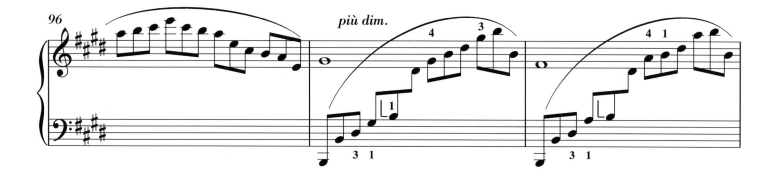

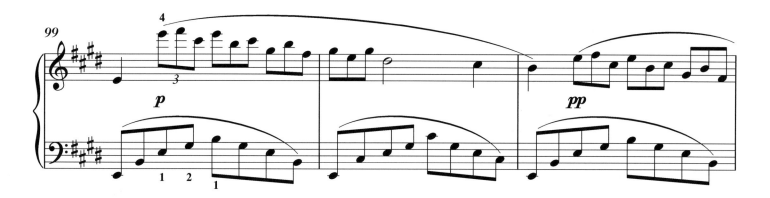

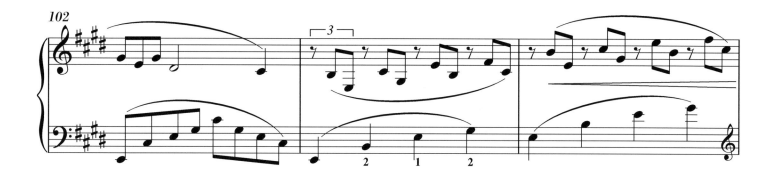

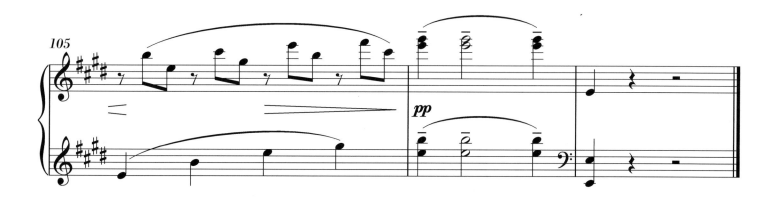

Deuxième Arabesque

Claude Debussy
L. 66, No. 2

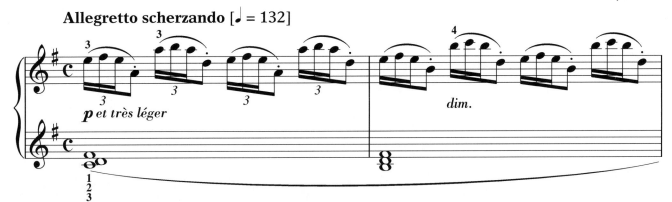

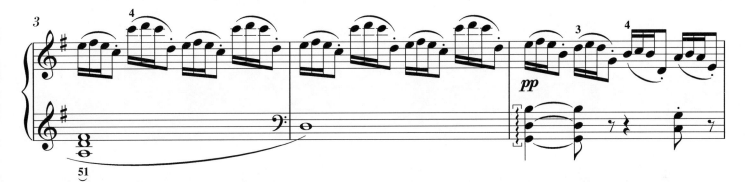

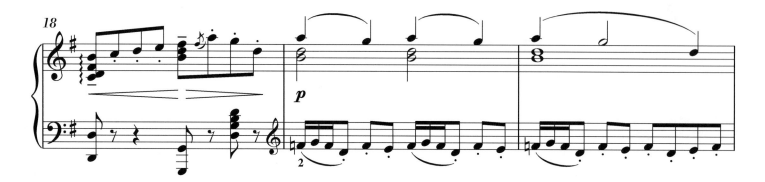

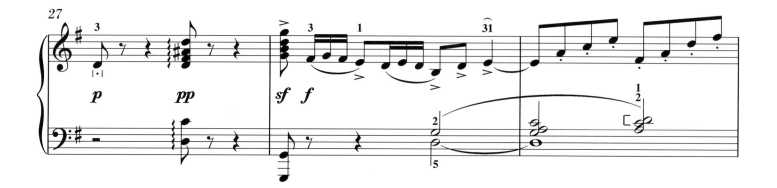

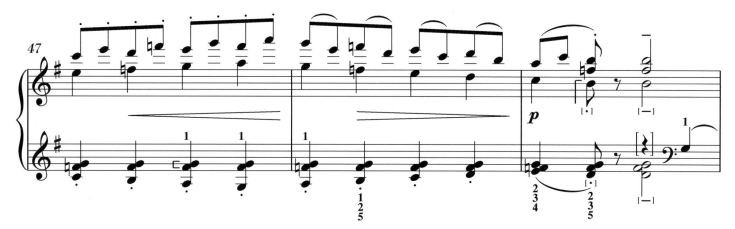

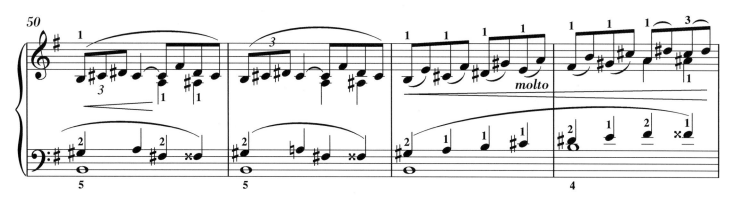

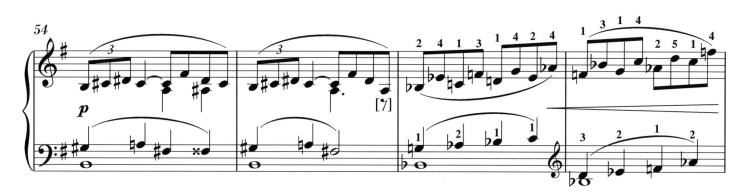

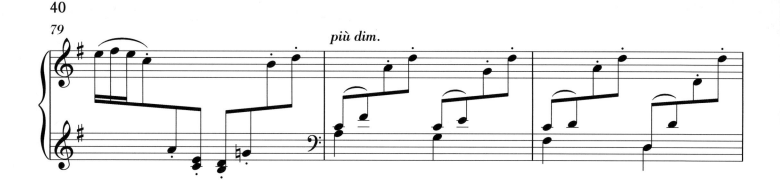

Meno mosso

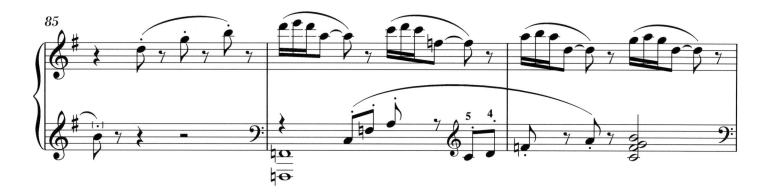

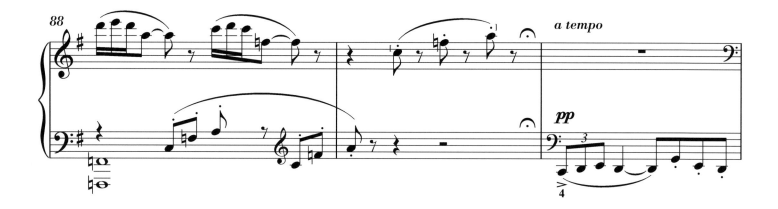

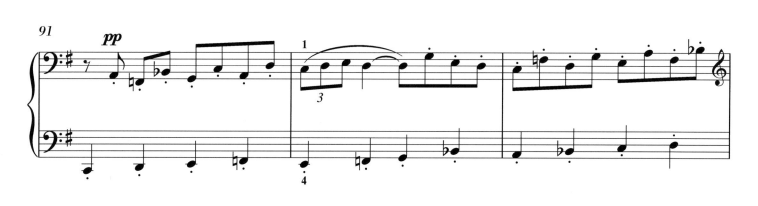

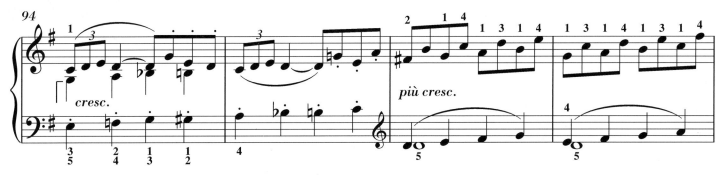

Rêverie

Claude Debussy
L. 68

Andantino, sans lenteur [♩ = 120]

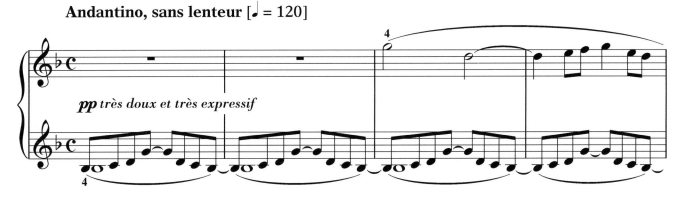

pp *très doux et très expressif*

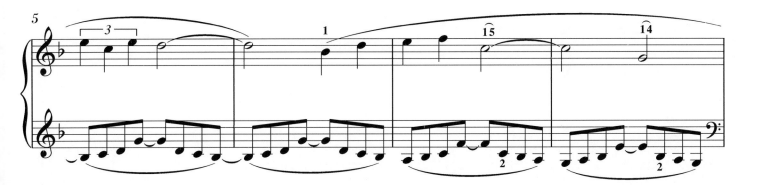

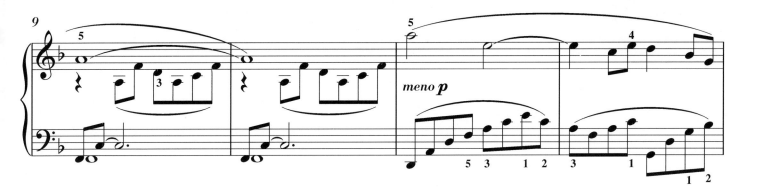

meno *p*

mf

dim.

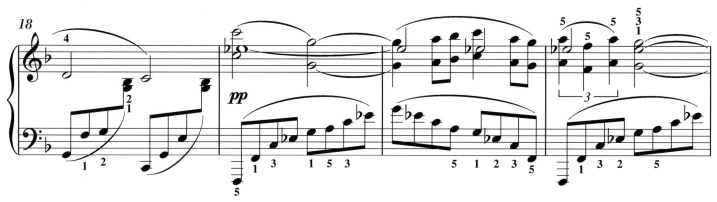

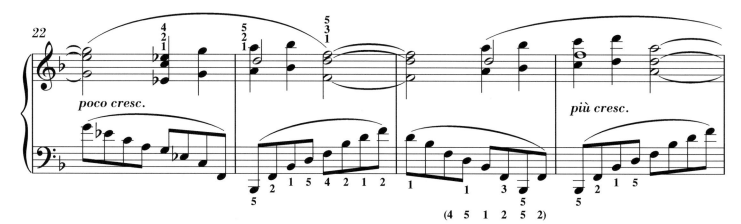

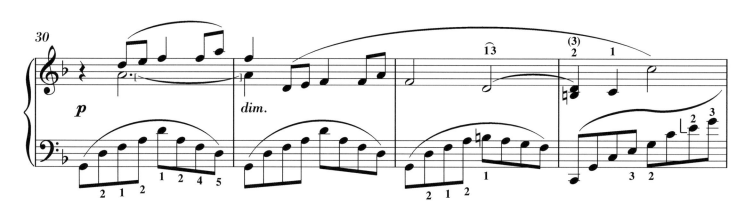

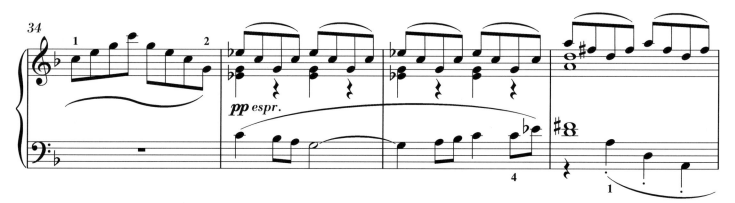

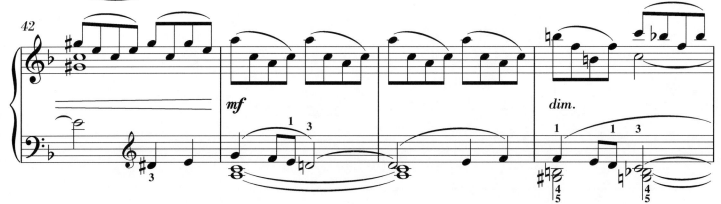

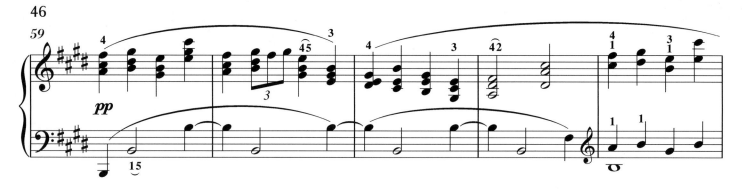

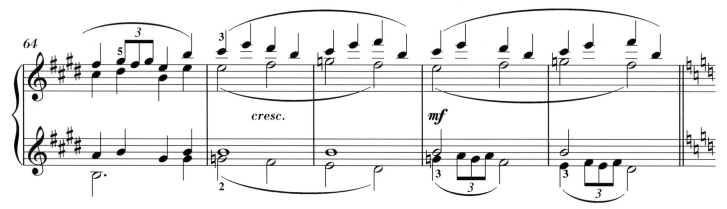

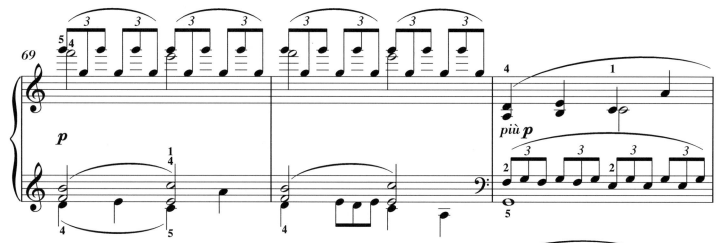

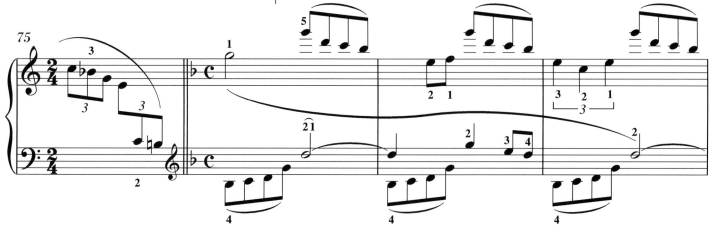

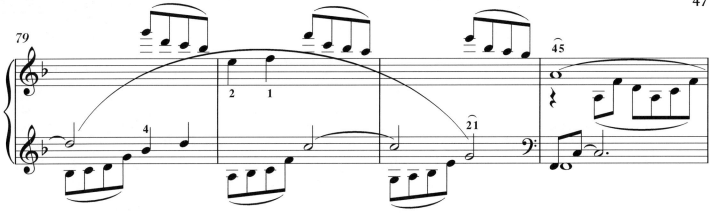

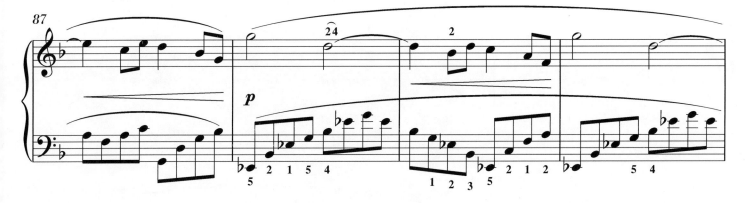

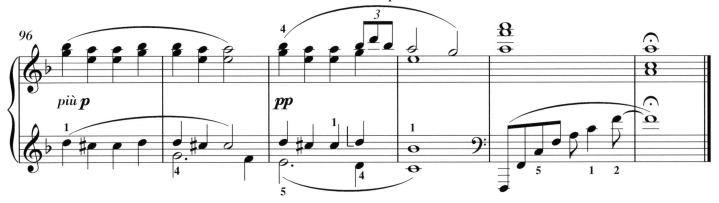

Clair de lune

from *Suite bergamasque*

Claude Debussy
L. 75, No. 3

Andante très expressif [♩. = 46]

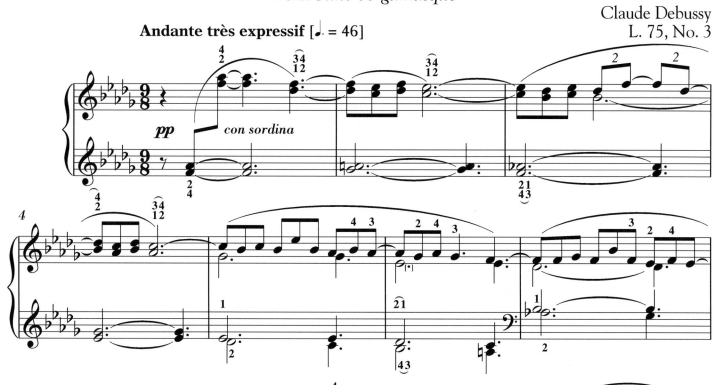

Tempo rubato

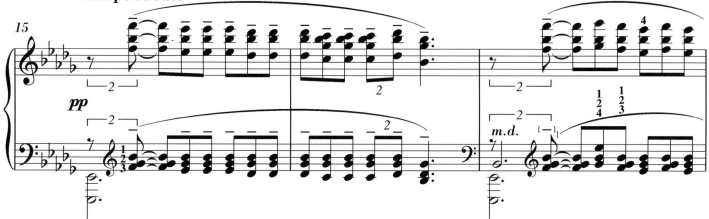

peu à peu cresc. et animé

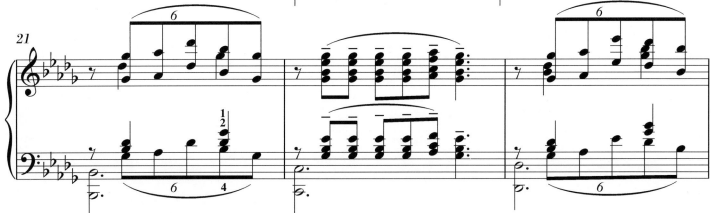

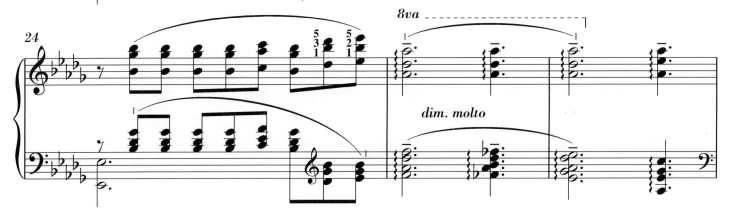

8va

dim. molto

Un poco mosso

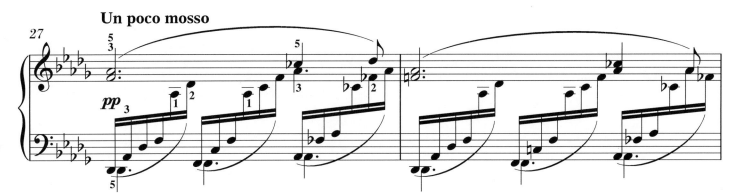

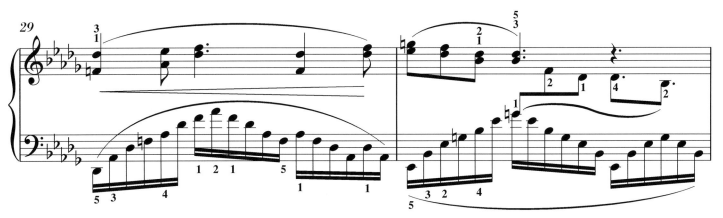

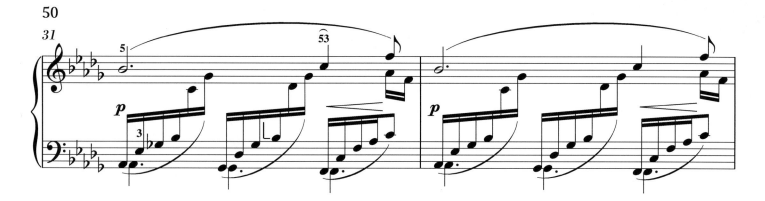

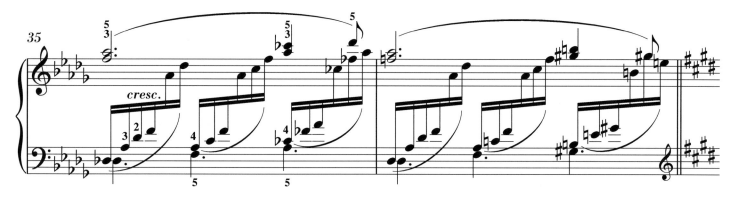

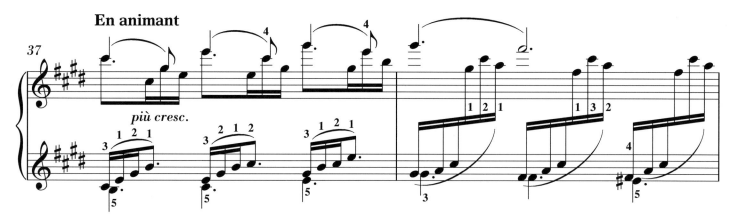

En animant

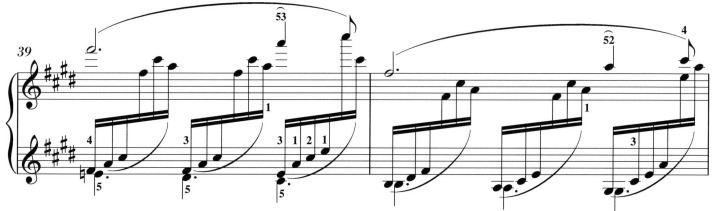

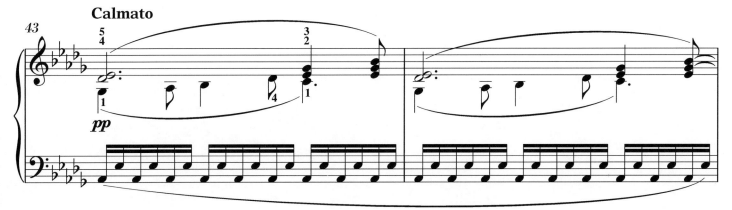

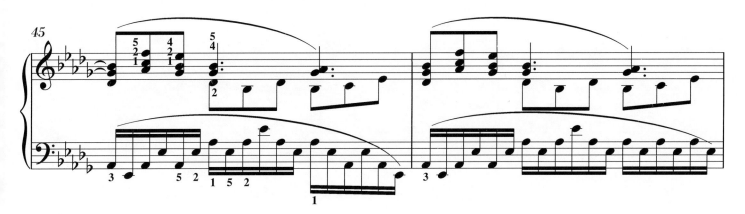

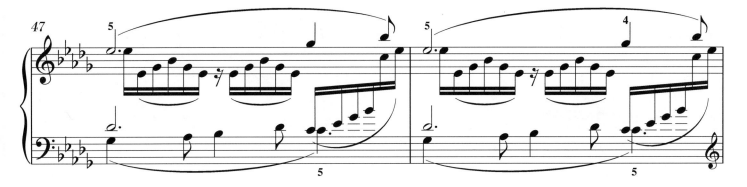

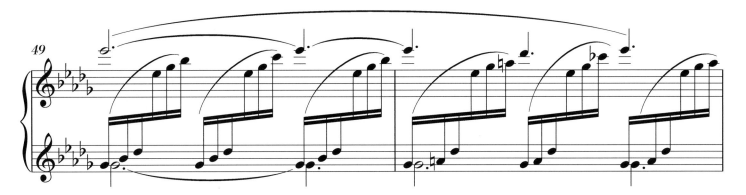

a Tempo I

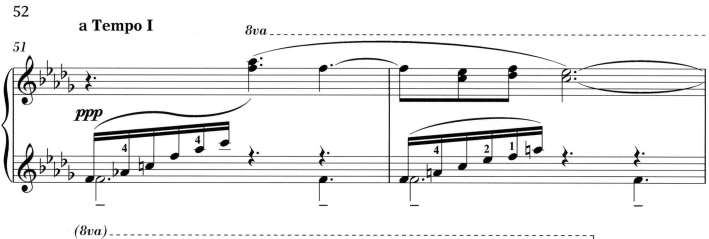

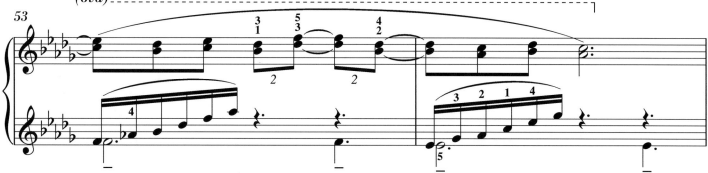

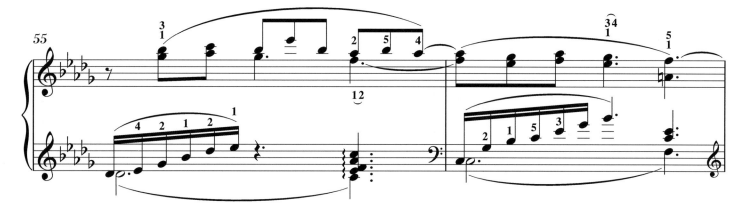

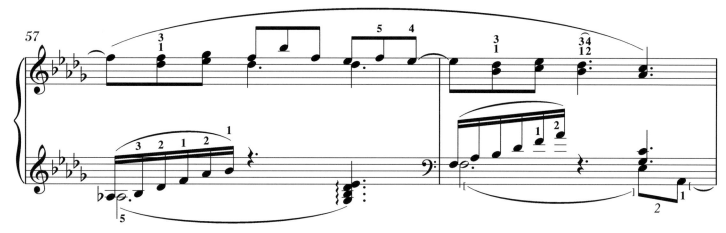

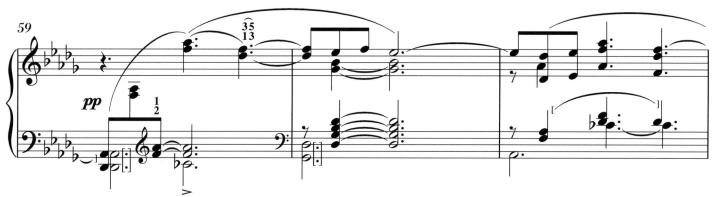

pp *morendo jusqu'à la fin*

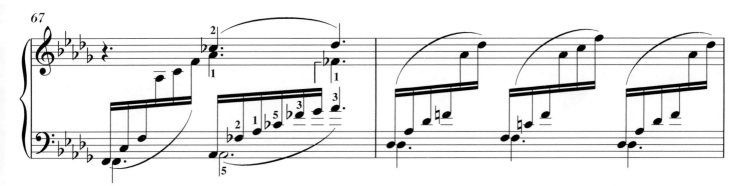

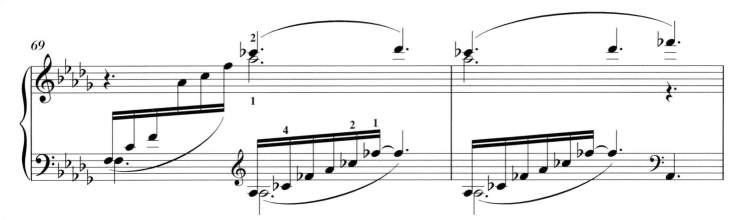

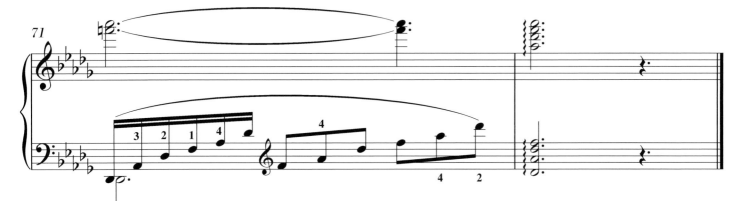

GLOSSARY OF FRENCH TERMS

FRENCH	ENGLISH
au Mouvt (au mouvement)	a tempo
Augmentez progressivement	crescendo progressively
Cédez	gradually slowing
Comme un écho de la phrase entendue précédemment	like an echo of the phrase heard previously
Dans la sonorité du début	with the resonant sonority of the beginning
Dans une brume doucement sonore	in a gently resonant haze
dans une expression allant grandissant	with a growing grandness
doux et expressif	sweet and expressive
Doux et fluide	sweet and fluid
En animant	becoming animated
en diminuant	diminishing
et très léger	and very light
expressif et concentré	expressive and focused (thoughtful)
Flottant et sourd	floating and muffled
marqué	marked
morendo jusqu'à la fin	dying until the end
Mouvt (Mouvement)	a tempo
Murmuré et en retenant peu à peu	murmuring and rallentando little by little

FRENCH	ENGLISH
peu à peu cresc. et animé	little by little louder and animated
Peu à peu sortant de la brume	little by little emerging from the mist
Profondément calme	profoundly calm
retenu	held back
sans lenteur	without slowness
sans lourdeur	without heaviness
sans nuances	without nuances
Sans presser	without getting faster
sans rigueur	without strictness (flexible)
Sonore sans dureté	resonant without harshness
Très calme et doucement expressif	very calm and tenderly expressive
très doux	very sweet
très doux et très expressif	very sweet and expressive
très expressif	very expressive
très leger	very light
très peu	very little
très rythmé	very rhythmic
Un peu animé	a little animated
Un peu moins lent	a little less slow
un peu moins vite	a little less quick
Un peu retenu	a little held back

ABOUT THE EDITOR

CHRISTOPHER HARDING

Christopher Harding is on the artist faculty of the University of Michigan, School of Music, Theatre, and Dance. He has performed internationally and across the United States, generating enthusiasm and impressing audiences and critics alike with his substantive interpretations and pianistic mastery. He has given frequent solo, concerto, and chamber music performances in venues as far flung as the Kennedy Center and Phillips Collection in Washington DC, Suntory Hall in Tokyo, the National Theater Concert Hall in Taipei, the Jack Singer Concert Hall in Calgary, and halls and festival appearances in Newfoundland and Israel. His concerto performances have included concerts with the National Symphony and the Saint Louis Symphony Orchestras, the San Angelo and Santa Barbara Symphonies, and the Tokyo City Philharmonic, working with such conductors as Taijiro Iimori, Gisele Ben-Dor, Fabio Machetti, Randall Craig Fleisher, John DeMain, Ron Spiegelman, Daniel Alcott, and Darryl One, among others. His chamber music and duo collaborations have included internationally renowned artists such as Karl Leister, András Adorján, and members of the St. Lawrence and Ying String Quartets, in addition to frequent projects with his distinguished faculty colleagues at the University of Michigan. He has recorded two solo discs and one chamber music disc for the Brevard Classics label.

Professor Harding has presented master classes and lecture recitals in universities across the United States and Asia, as well as in Israel and Canada. Additionally, he has extensively toured China under the auspices of the U.S. State Department, and was in residence at the Sichuan Conservatory of Music as a Fulbright Senior Specialist at the invitation of the American Consulate in Chengdu, China.

Mr. Harding was born of American parents in Munich, Germany, and raised in Northern Virginia. He holds degrees and Performer's Certificates from the Eastman School of Music and the Indiana University School of Music. His collegiate studies were with Menahem Pressler and Nelita True. Prior to college, he worked for ten years with Milton Kidd at the American University Department of Performing Arts Preparatory Division, where he was trained in the traditions of Tobias Matthay. He has taken twenty-five first prizes in national and international competitions, and in 1999 was awarded the special Mozart Prize at the Cleveland International Piano Competition, given for the best performance of a composition by Mozart.